VOLCANOES & EARTHQUAKES, WHAT & WHY?: 2ND GRADE SCIENCE SERIES

SPEEDY
PUBLISHING

Speedy Publishing LLC
40 E. Main St. #1156
Newark, DE 19711
www.speedypublishing.com

Earthquakes and volcanic eruptions happen at the boundaries between plates.

VOLCANOES

Volcanoes are openings in the Earth's surface. When they are active they can let ash, gas and hot magma escape in sometimes violent and spectacular eruptions.

Volcanoes
are formed when
magma from within the
Earth's upper mantle works its
way to the surface. It erupts to
form lava flows and ash deposits.
As the volcano continues to
erupt, it will get bigger
and bigger.

Lava and Magma are both molten rock. Magma is liquid rock inside a volcano. Lava is liquid rock that flows out of a volcano.

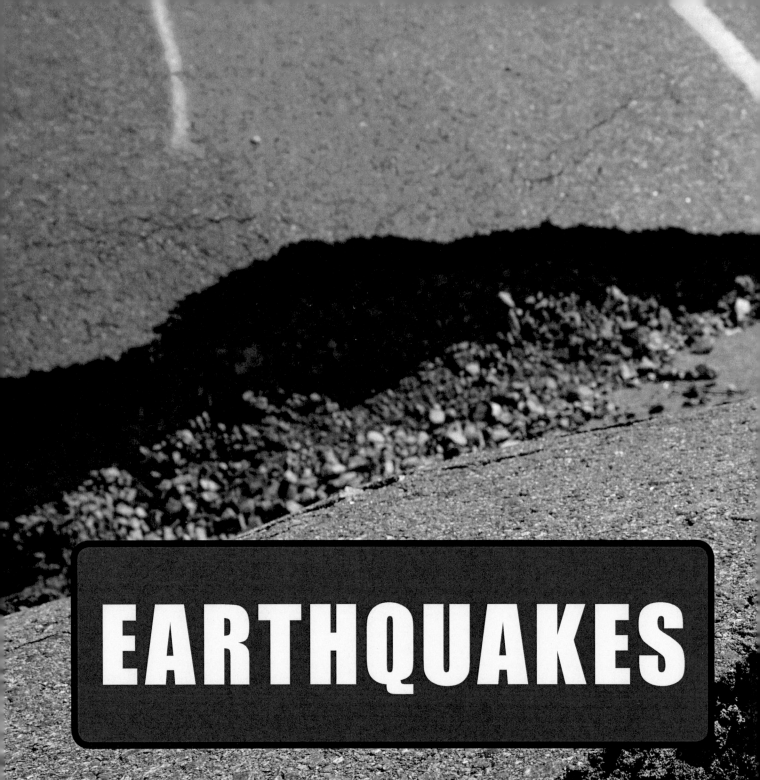

EARTHQUAKES

Earthquakes are the rumblings, shaking or rolling of the earth's surface. They are the Earth's natural means of releasing stress. More than a million earthquakes shake the world each year.

There are about 20 plates along the surface of the earth. The plates constantly move. Earthquakes happen when a plate scrapes, bumps, or drags along another plate.

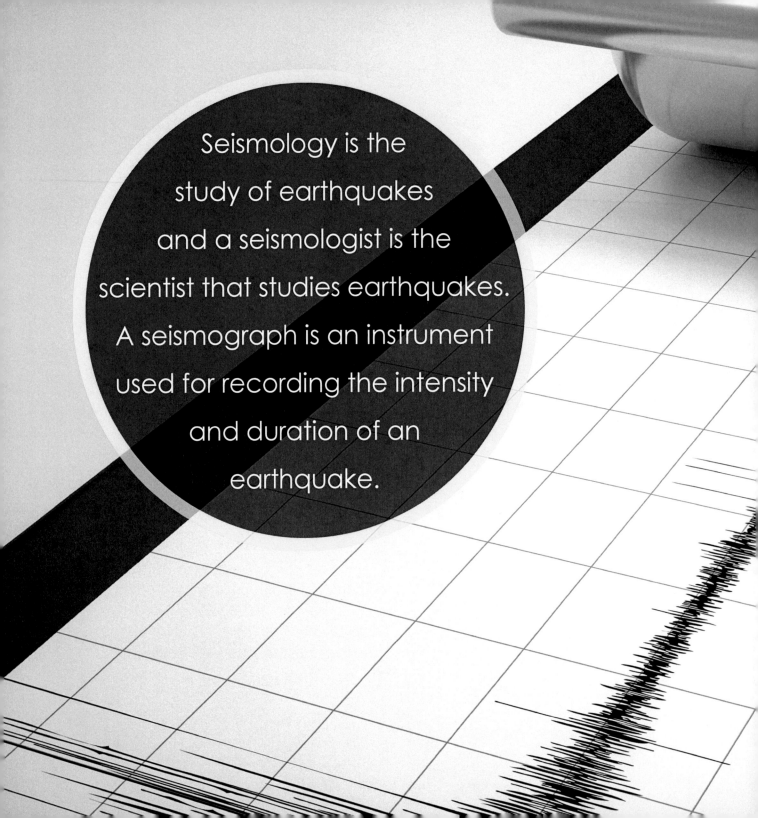

Seismology is the study of earthquakes and a seismologist is the scientist that studies earthquakes. A seismograph is an instrument used for recording the intensity and duration of an earthquake.

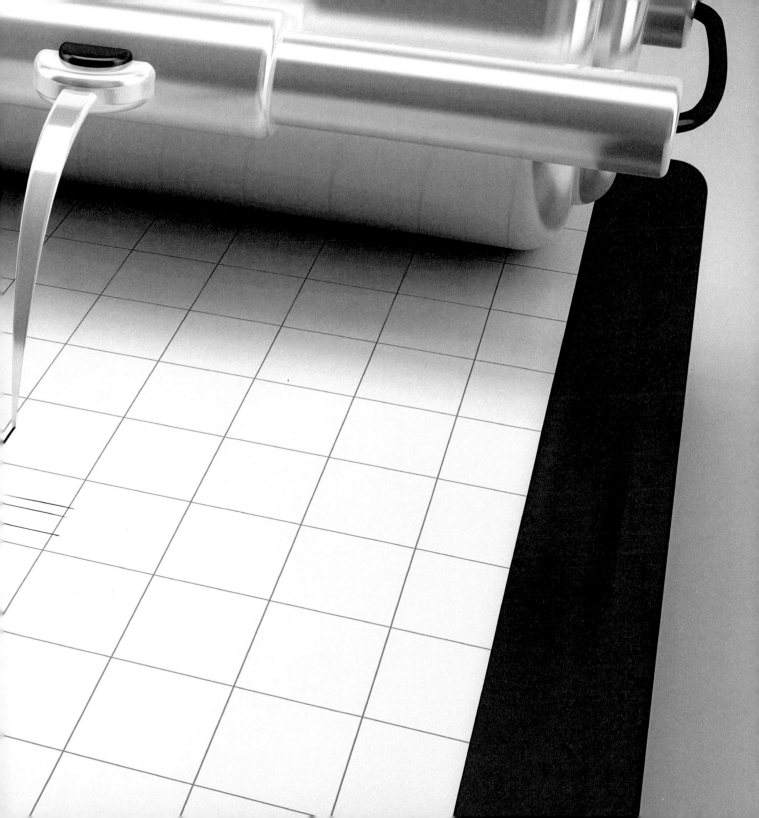

Made in the USA
San Bernardino, CA
23 May 2017